Partners in the Divine Dance of Our Three Person'd God

Shaun McCarty, S.T.

Paulist Press
New York/Mahwah, New Jersey

Cover/book design and interior illustrations by Nicholas T. Markell.

Library of Congress Cataloging-in-Publication Data

McCarty, Shaun, 1929–
    Partners in the divine dance of our three Person'd God / Shaun McCarty.
        p.   cm.–(IlluminationBooks)
    Includes bibliographical references.
    ISBN 0-8091-3655-4 (alk. paper)
    1. Trinity–Prayer-books and devotions–English. 2. Catholic Church–Prayer-books and devotions–English. I. Title. II. Series: IlluminationBooks.
BT113.M33   1996
248.3–dc20   96-13383
                                                              CIP

Published by Paulist Press
997 Macarthur Boulevard
Mahwah, NJ 07430

Printed and bound in the
United States of America

Contents

Dedication

To Sister "Sarah"—
a senior partner in prayer,
now in the bosom of Abraham—
who continues to accompany me
in the divine dance

IlluminationBooks

A Foreword

*I*lluminationBooks bring to light wonderful ideas, helpful information, and sound spirituality in concise, illustrative, readable, and eminently practical works on topics of current concern. Learning from stress; interior peace; personal prayer; biblical awareness; walking with others in darkness; appreciating the love already in our lives; spiritual discernment; uncovering helpful psychological antidotes for our tendency to worry too much at times; and important guides to improving interpersonal relations are only several of the areas which will be covered in this series.

The goal of each IlluminationBook, then, is to provide great ideas, helpful steps, and needed inspiration in small volumes. Each book offers a new beginning for the reader to explore possibilities and embrace practicalities which can be employed in everyday life.

In today's busy and anxious world, Illumination-Books are meant to provide a source of support—without requiring an inordinate amount of time or prior preparation. Each small work stands on its own. Hopefully, the information provided not only will be nourishing in itself but also will encourage further exploration in the area.

One is obviously never done learning. With every morsel of wisdom each of these books provides, the goal is to keep the process of seeking knowledge ongoing even during busy times, when sitting down with a larger work is impossible or undesirable.

However, more than information (as valuable as it is), at the base of each work in the series is a deep sense of *hope* that is based on a belief in the beautiful statement made by Jesus to his disciples and in turn to us: "You are my friends" (Jn 15:15).

As "friends of God" we must seek the presence of the Lord in ourselves, in others, in silence and solitude, in nature, and in daily situations. IlluminationBooks are designed to provide implicit and explicit opportunities to appreciate this reality in new ways. So, it is in this spirit that this book and the other ones in the series are offered to you.
                                                    —*Robert J. Wicks*
                                    General Editor, IlluminationBooks

Introduction

*B*atter my heart, three person'd God; for you
            As yet but knocke, breathe, shine, and seek to mend;
That I may rise and stand, o'erthrow mee, and bend
Your force, to breake, blowe, burn and make mee new.
I, like an usurpt towne, to another due,
Labour to admit you, but Oh, to no end,
Reason, your viceroy in mee, mee should defend,
But is captiv'd, and proves weak or untrue.

Yet dearly I love you, and would be
       loved faine,
But I am betrothed unto your enemies:
Divorce mee, untie, or brake that knot
       again,
Take mee to you, imprison mee, for I
Except you enthrall mee, never shall be free,
Nor ever chaste, except you ravish mee.

—John Donne
Divine Poems, 1633

Hardly the bland, abstract, irrelevant language of more modern descriptions concerning the distinctively Christian mystery of our belief, the most holy Trinity! Rather, these are passionate verses of older vintage that speak of a living, concerned, dynamic God of human experience. They come from the heart of a seventeenth-century Anglican clergyman who could address his God with the ardor of a lover. He scorned the easy platitude and the smooth, empty phrase. Perhaps we would do well to capture some of the fire of his language in addressing the triune God of love in terms that would make this God more relevant and alive for many Christians today.

Many, from both pew and pulpit, would agree today that the mystery of the Trinity has little relevance for their lives and prayer. For the majority of practicing Christians, at least in our own highly individualistic culture, this core mystery of our Christian faith is more of a mystifying formula than an energizing force. The mystery of the Trinity, as traditionally presented, hardly speaks to human persons made in God's image and likeness. It does little to shape Christian development as passionate and loving persons called to grow in community.

It seems clear that there is a need to speak about and to pray the mystery of the Trinity in ways more dynamic and related to the lives of ordinary believers today. This is an effort to address this need. It is born of the conviction that, as Christians, our language, lives and prayer ought to be rooted in this distinctively Christian mystery of the most holy Trinity.

Certainly doctrine and creeds are important for expressing mysteries of faith. But symbols, stories and ritual enable us to pray them in more vivid and imaginative ways. If doctrine and creeds are the prose of truth, then symbol, story and ritual are the poetry. They speak to the heart as well as the head and can save doctrines and creeds from blandness. What follows is an attempt to wed head and heart in glorifying the triune God. The heart more than the head is home for the divine indwelling presence.

This little volume is a modest effort to shed some light and to enkindle some heat in fostering a deeper and richer relationship for ordinary believers with our three person'd God. My hope is to invite the reader toward a "devotional knowledge" of the mystery that may allow it to be more relevant to Christian life and prayer today. Consider this a prayer companion for spending some quality time getting to know and to experience more deeply the mystery of the holy and undivided Trinity.

The Greek word used to describe the living and unified presence of the three divine persons in all their loving activities is *perichoresis*. It literally means "dancing around." Some of the early church fathers punned on this great technical word. They imagined the Trinity as a dancing of reality—the one and the many—a plurality coming together in the harmony and beauty of the dance. We best reflect their divine life and activity when we live as they do, as "partners" in the divine dance—in spiritual community with them and with one another.

By "spiritual community" I mean the experience of communion with others lived in the image and likeness of the triune God, that is, as a unity-in-diversity engaged in mutual dialogue and selfless love. Perhaps this notion of spiritual community is more aptly expressed in metaphor. A former student caught the notion with the metaphor of dance:

> The gesture that expresses spiritual community for me is the dance. What is more hospitable than the invitation to dance, an invitation to intimacy? And for those moments...of tentativeness and risk, there is total commitment to the partner, sensitivity to each other's gentlest move, and all in response to the music that is drawing us both...reverberating, echoing...

And I will hesitate, and you will stumble, as we try to catch again the rhythm—and we may reverse roles as I count a little and lead where you couldn't find your way for a minute. But even if you step on my toes, I can't sit down because the dancers and the dance are one—and the whole world needs us to dance and to invite them out on the floor with us, all hearing the same music and responding to it in our own ways. Or is it that the whole of creation is dancing and we've just caught the music?[1]

This is an invitation to become partners with our three person'd God in their divine dance. It's important to remember that a partner is someone you work with on a big thing that neither of you can do alone. Partners dance, not march together. Time to catch the music!

I will suggest some ways by which we might read, reflect, pray, live and love our way more deeply into a consciousness of the indwelling Trinity. Some suggestions and questions for reflection are woven into the text. They are meant to engage the reader with the text. My hope and prayer is that our journey together will bring a bit more passion and relevance to our devotion to the three person'd God.

Chapter One
Providing Hospitality for Our Partner God

At the outset, I'd like to offer the reader some suggestions for creating a welcoming environment for communing with God. If any fit, fine; if not, pray as you can!

(1) *Find time.* Find some room in your life for unambiguous time for the Lord. Reorder priorities if necessary. Let your prayer fit sensibly into the rhythm of your life, but consider it prime time. There are two kinds of time: *chronos* and *kairos*. *Chronos* is time on the clock and calendar that we keep (or that keeps us!). *Kairos* is the time of readiness when we can sense the "right" moment. I like to think of *chronos* time as more our time and *kairos* time

as more God's. The "right" time for prayer may come as unexpectedly as a rainy or snowy day when previous plans have to be canceled.

(2) *Find space.* Find a privileged place where you can be quiet and relatively undisturbed and uninhibited in your response to God's word. We've come to appreciate the subtle power for good or ill that environment can have in shaping values, attitudes and behaviors. The same holds true for finding the right "ecology" for prayer. That will vary for different people. For me, sacred space is a place set apart from the rush and noise and busy-ness of everyday. It's a kind of "hole in the donut" of a day, week, month or year. It's where I can "waste time" without guilt by watching sunrises and sunsets, birds and people, by listening to sounds of nature or good music. My sacred space is where I can go fishing, even without a pole. It's where I can get in harmony with the flow of life. It's where I can claim my "celibate core." "Celibate" in this context has nothing to do with being unmarried. It means "alone, whole and healthy." There is a "celibate core," an inner sanctuary of the soul in each of us, regardless of marital status. It's where we can become better acquainted with ourselves and discover a better self to give to others. In short, sacred space is where we can let Jesus' promise of a more abundant life find fulfillment.

A good example of sacred space is a *poustinia.*[2] That's the Russian word for "desert." It's a place for silence, solitude, penance and prayer offered in a spirit of love. Here pilgrims journey to quiet space to commune

with their indwelling God. Though *poustinias* occupy simple physical space, they are essentially space within the heart. They are compatible with presence in the marketplace to which one can bring a *poustinia* of the heart.

One enters a *poustinia* as a beggar into the unknown to listen to God. This calls for an "emptying of self" so as to pursue purity of heart. Though an experience of solitude, there is a communal dimension to it. The whole of humanity accompanies the one who enters the *poustinia*. One who dwells there aspires to a cosmic tenderness toward all creatures. Hospitality is characteristic of this sacred space. One remains available for the service of another in need. A *poustinia* is always left unlatched as a sign of availability.

(3) *Be all there.* Bring your whole self to prayer—spirit, mind and body. Of the three, body seems the most neglected in prayer. Certainly bowing, kneeling, folding hands, extending arms, striking the breast, prostrating the body and the like have been traditional ways of bringing the body to prayer. In addition, you might also consider starting prayer with stretching, deep breathing or some other discipline of bodily movement. It's also helpful for deep listening to assume an attentive, but relaxed bodily posture. In the course of prayer, you may feel moved to dance!

(4) *Listen.* Be aware of your senses of sight, sound, smell, taste and touch. Bring them to your prayer too, but focus your attention in a relaxed way on what the Lord has to say to you at this time. Be in touch, too, with yourself

on the inside—your preoccupations (problems, projects, people, etc.); your feelings (mood, anxieties, joys, etc.). Be especially attentive to where you feel most helpless and vulnerable. It's likely that's where you're most open to grace! Finally, be aware of God's presence and power in your life at this moment. Place each care and anxiety in the arms of Jesus to carry. After you let go of your own burdens, express a willingness to help carry the burdens of others. Invite the Lord to speak to your heart. Ask for the grace to hear and to respond.

(5) *Try praying with an icon.* Icons are like "windows into mystery." They are the opposite of idols which stop short of or substitute for the living God. Icons are a form of visual theology that give artistic expression to faith through the celebration of form and color. The eastern churches in particular have chosen icons as a way of expressing the vision of God in a spiritual art form. They portray spiritual, not physical bodies (1 Cor 15:44). Based on the mystery of the incarnation, icons assume that Christ is the icon of the invisible God (Col 1:15) and that the entire visible world is an image of the kingdom of God. They contain a doctrine of God's image in creation and invite us to enter into the action of God's self-disclosure.

As invitations and aids to prayer, icons are meant to carry us beyond the materials of which they are made. They nourish a spirituality of presence and receptivity more than one of analysis, thought or action. Icons are meant to lead us to a contemplation of the divine presence that, in turn, leads to illumination and transfiguration in our own lives. Icon prayer calls us to see the vision of a transfigured world under God's reign. Contemplating an icon is a way of entering more deeply into the mystery of divine life while remaining fully engaged in the struggles of this life. They picture not the ordinary, but the divine life behind the image.

Perhaps the best way to pray with an icon is to gaze at it receptively, bow the head and let it reveal the mystery of God-with-us. A reflective meditation on sacred scripture can help. Reading or hearing about icons is not enough. One must stay in silence before them. In so doing, such prayer can bring a knowledge of mind-in-the-heart.

(6) *Journal.* Writing in a journal is a way of being in inner dialogue with ourselves. For many it is an aid in gaining new perspectives, greater clarity and deeper self-understanding. Sometimes it's helpful to read aloud what is written—to allow the journal to "talk back." How can we know what we know or feel until we hear what we say? It can be especially helpful to set aside periodic times to review what we've written to note patterns of growth or "stuckness" on our respective journeys. It's also a way of "stringing the beads of past epiphanies."

(7) *Finish.* End your prayer time with an act of surrender of yourself to the Lord for the day and for the courage to make your life as you live it a validation of your prayer as you pray it. Be consoled in the assurance that "the Spirit, too, helps us in our weakness, for we do not know how to pray as we ought; but the Spirit himself

makes intercession for us with groanings that cannot be expressed in speech" (Rom 8:26).

(8) *Later.* Share your prayer life with another or others on a consistent basis. Spiritual guides or companions can help you to identify and to clarify how you might grow in your relationship with God. It's also a way of sharing your own "good news!"

Chapter Two

A Mysterious Threesome

*P*ermit me to share one of my favorite "trinitarian" stories. I'm told it's as ancient as Augustine and as recent as Anthony de Mello. I've heard there is even a Sufi version. Perhaps the most literate rendition is from the Russian (sometimes iconoclast!) writer, Leo Tolstoy. Published as "The Three Hermits" in 1885, his source was probably the legend form that came to him in an oral version of the tale. With apologies to Tolstoy and the others, I offer my own adapted version that I've entitled "A Mysterious Threesome."

Many years ago a newly appointed Russian archbishop was sailing with pilgrims to visit the various churches in his see which was comprised mainly of islands and archipelagos. As he sauntered among the pilgrims on deck, he noticed one of them pointing to the bare speck of an island on the horizon. Drawing closer, he overheard the group speaking of three ancient and holy hermits who lived there and who spent their time mostly in silence. "When approached by outsiders," one pilgrim remarked, "they merely say, 'Have mercy on us.'"

As the ship drew closer, the archbishop, sure enough, spotted the three through a spyglass. They were standing near a large rock formation—one tall, another a bit shorter, and the third, even smaller. The archbishop asked the captain to put him ashore. The captain suggested that it would be a waste of time as the men were old, foolish and spoke poorly. But the archbishop insisted. So the captain relented, trimmed his sails, dropped anchor and put the churchman, clad in his episcopal robes, ashore in a small dinghy.

As the oarsmen drew near the island, they saw the hermits up close. The tall one was clad in a piece of sackcloth; the one somewhat shorter wore a torn coat; the ancient little one was clothed in a threadbare cassock. As the boat approached, they stood together holding each other by the hand.

As the archbishop disembarked in regal attire, the hermits bowed low and he blessed them. They bowed even lower.

"I have heard," the visitor began, "that you are godly men seeking salvation and praying for people. I am here, by God's grace, to tend my flock and, if I can, to give you servants of God instruction. Tell me how you serve God and seek salvation."

Each of the three looked to the other and, finally, the eldest smiled and said, "We don't know, servant of God, how to serve God. We only serve and feed ourselves."

Somewhat dismayed, the archbishop queried further, "How, then, do you pray to God?"

After some hesitation, the eldest again answered: "We pray thus: 'Three of us, three of you, Lord, have mercy.'"

With a bemused smile, the distinguished visitor replied: "I can see that you want to please God, but do not know how to serve him. You must have heard of the Holy Trinity, but you pray in the wrong way. Don't you know the Lord's Prayer?"

The hermits' faces fell in shame and sadness as they confessed, "We never heard of the Lord's Prayer."

"I know now why God sent me to you today!" said the archbishop. "I'm here to teach you the proper way to pray."

He then proceeded to have the hermits repeat after him verses of the Lord's Prayer. With great difficulty they repeated after him first one verse, then another together with the previous verse and so on until evening. Finally they were able to recite the entire prayer by themselves.

Amidst more deep bows and words of thanks, the archbishop bade them farewell and returned to the ship as the hermits continued to shout in chorus the verses of the Lord's Prayer.

Back on board, the ship weighed anchor and again set sail. The archbishop, immensely pleased with himself for having taught these holy men to pray, rested in the stern of the ship and watched the tiny island fade from sight.

By this time, the pilgrims were asleep and all was quiet on deck as the archbishop kept gazing at the sea in the direction of the island. Suddenly he saw something glowing on the sea and moving in the direction of the ship. It was too high in the water for a fish, too close to the water for a bird, too small for another ship.

Moving swiftly to the helmsman, the confused cleric shouted, "Look!"

The helmsman, dumbfounded, shouted back, "My lord, the hermits are chasing the ship over the sea!"

This awakened the pilgrims who rushed to the stern. In awe, they all saw the hermits running on the water, waving their arms, bidding the ship to stop. When the threesome drew close, they climbed aboard, raised their heads and spoke in unison: "We have forgotten, servant of God, your teaching! As long as we kept repeating it, we remembered it. But then we stopped to rest for an hour. When we started again, one word escaped us and everything fell apart. Please teach us again."

The chastened archbishop crossed himself, bowed toward the hermits and said: "My dear, holy men, go back and pray: 'Three of us, three of you, Lord, have mercy.' It is not for me to teach you. Pray for this sinner." And the archbishop bowed to the ground again before the hermits who turned and ran happily back over the sea to their island hermitage, leaving a radiance in their wake.

I find this folk tale a healthy caution in "teaching" people to pray. We need to assume that the presence and power of an all-loving God are with people before "teachers" come on the scene. Many may simply need help in becoming more aware of this.

The story also speaks to me about how a loving community provides the essential communal dimension for all Christian prayer. In their unity of purpose and loving diversity, the three reflect something of God's "image and likeness." Their prayer begins with their human experience of being together.

The story accentuates that prayer is not limited to formal, structured prayers. It is important that we pray "from where we are," but allow ourselves always to be challenged to the "more." I would wager that learning the Lord's Prayer gave them another way of praying "Three of us, three of you!" In that marvelously trinitarian prayer, it is in the power of the Spirit and in company with Jesus that we are enabled to confess Jesus as Lord and address God as "our" *Abba*, Father.

The three chasing the ship across the sea conjures up for me an image of the mystery of God's power at work affecting our human condition and empowering our deepest desires for union with God.

• Does the story speak to you in any way of our being in God's image and likeness?

• How is your prayer trinitarian?

• What has helped shape it that way?

Chapter Three
Embracing the Mystery

*L*est I share the arrogance of the arch-bishop in trying to "teach" people to pray, it should be clear that what we are most sure of concerning the Trinity is that it is a mystery to be lived, not a problem or puzzle to be solved. I believe we best approach mystery with "learned ignorance" and by knowing that God is hidden in "bright darkness." Paradox and silence are the language of mystery.

The word "mystery" literally means "hidden." In a faith context, the term refers to truth that has been revealed and invites entry. Blaise Pascal once said, "A religion which does not affirm that God is hidden is not true." In our pursuit of devotional knowledge of the Trinity, we begin and end with the mystery of God.

Mystery defies efforts to domesticate it by subjecting it to analysis, predictability or other forms of control. It is knowable, but not by way of intellectual comprehension. We can have some ideas about it. That's theology. But real knowledge is by way of *experience*, that is, by allowing ourselves to be drawn into mystery. To "know" the Trinity is know ourselves as drawn into the mystery of it; to be participants in it rather than mere spectators apart from it.

The reality of the presence of God in the biblical experience of Old and New Testament figures has always been elusive. Moses sensed God's presence and heard God's voice in a burning bush. Elijah found God in a gentle whispering breeze. God invites our reach, but eludes our grasp. The verses of Robert Browning say it well: "Oh that a man's reach should exceed his grasp/Or what's a heaven for?" Michelangelo's fresco, "The Creation," on the ceiling of the Sistine Chapel captures human limits in color. In it, the finger of man reaches for, but doesn't quite grasp the finger of God. Mystery demands that we respect God's otherness while seeking God's closeness. On the one hand, we shouldn't make God inaccessible; on the other, we dare not make God too much into our own image and to our own liking.

In his charming little best-seller,[3] Robert Fulghum reminisces while watching the neighborhood kids play hide-and-seek. He asks:

Did you have a kid in your neighborhood who always hid so good, nobody could find him? We did. After a while we would give up on him and go off, leaving him to rot wherever he was. Sooner or later he would show up all mad because we didn't keep looking for him. And we would get mad back because he wasn't playing the game the way it was supposed to be played. "There's hiding and there's *finding*," we'd say. And he would say it was hide-and-seek, not hide-and-give up and we'd all yell about who made the rules...No matter what, though, the next time he would hide too good again. He's probably still hidden somewhere, for all I know...

As he watches, Fulghum spies a kid under a pile of leaves in his yard and the others are about to give up on him. He considers telling the others where the kid is hiding or setting the leaves on fire to drive him out. He finally settles for yelling out the window, "Get found, kid!" and scares him so bad, he starts crying and runs home to tell his mother.

Better than hide-and-seek, Fulghum says, he likes the game called "Sardines" in which the person who is "It" hides and everybody goes looking for him or her. When each one finds the kid who is It, he or she gets in and they hide together. Pretty soon someone laughs and everybody gets found.

Fulghum goes on to say he thinks God is a

"Sardines" player and will be found the same way everybody gets found in "Sardines"—by the sound of laughter of those heaped together at the end. "To all those who have hid too good," he says, "Get Found, Kid! Olly-olly-oxen-free."

God is "It," hidden in plain sight, and wanting to be found! From another view, it may be more proper to say that, in our search for God, God finds *us* more than we find God! If God is a "Sardines" player, then doesn't that once again speak of the communal context that is proper for Christian prayer? Perhaps a key to embracing mystery is not to hide in isolation!

We glorify God on God's terms, not our own. This presumes that faith, not reason, is the proper way of embracing the mystery of God. What we say about God or how we image God is by way of analogy. That means that what we say about and how we picture God is more unlike than like God. God is *like* a good shepherd, a mother hen, a farmer sowing seed, but God is not confined by these images.

Embracing the mystery of the Trinity primarily involves allowing ourselves to be caught up in the mystery receptively, patiently, reverently and with abandon. Silence more than words seems the proper language for mystery. And yet, words are born of silence. We dare to speak the ineffable! Another paradox?

• What are some of your favorite images for God?

• Do you find God playful? Can you give a "for instance"?

• How does silence help you grapple with mystery?

Chapter Four

Devotional Knowledge
of Mystery

I *wrote earlier that our quest is for "devotional knowledge" of the mystery of the Trinity. It's time I said what that means. By "devotional knowledge" I mean a knowledge that is more than ideas about someone or something. As "knowledge," it is the fruit of intimate and personal experience of another rather than the result of study. It's a quest guided by love rather than by intellectual curiosity. This knowledge is received not so much by the mind as by the heart. It comes more from the experience of knowing that I am loved than from knowing the other whom I love. This is a kind of knowledge*

"...hidden from the learned and the clever [that] you have revealed to the merest children" (Mt 11:25). It also has been given to disciples: "To you has been given a knowledge of the mysteries of the reign of God..." (Mt 13:11).

As "devotional," it is a knowledge that leads one to the service of God and is tested and nurtured by the expression of other acts of love.

Devotion

The word "devotion" comes from a Latin word that means "total dedication." In its original pagan usage, it referred to one who vowed to die for one's country. Christian writers found it an ideal expression of what our proper disposition toward God should be. Religious devotion is simply a willingness to praise and to serve God and others. No one has written more beautifully of devotion than St. Francis de Sales. He says:

> True love of God not only prompts us to do good, but also to do this carefully, frequently and promptly...Devotion is simply that spiritual agility and vivacity by which charity works in us or by aid of which we work quickly and lovingly... Charity and devotion differ no more...than does flame from the fire. Charity is spiritual fire and when it bursts into flame, it is called devotion.[4]

Often feelings accompany devotion; yet devotion is not ultimately measured by feelings. The real test of genuine devotion is its expression in other God-oriented acts such as commitment, service of others and sacrificial love. The opposite of devotion is lukewarmness.

As with all grace, God initiates devotion. It is God's grace, too, coupled with our desire that makes us receptive and responsive to God's initiatives. I like to think that God defines us more by our desires than our achievements, even the spiritual ones!

Devotional knowledge is practical, particular and personal.

It's *practical*. It leads to action that becomes real in ordinary, down-to-earth expressions of love that bring forth growth in others as well as in self. It enables us to say "yes" (or at least "sometimes!") to the question, "Is my life as I live it a validation of my prayer as I pray it?" This is not to say that prayer is merely a means to living a good life nor is it to "use" the gracious mysteries of faith as mere guides for practical living. Rather it is to say that living a truly devout life *in itself* gives glory to God!

Devotional knowledge is *particular*. It finds specific and concrete ways of giving our values flesh—visibility, audibility, tangibility. A devout person is not content with general and vague intentions. For example, if I pray, "Lord, be merciful to me, a sinner," can I name some of my sins? Or do I settle for being a "generic" sinner? If I acknowledge being gifted by the Spirit, can I name the gifts? If I can't name them, how can I develop and use them for extending God's reign? Devotional knowledge courts the "angel of specificity" and dismisses the "demon of generalization."

Devotional knowledge is *personal*. Personal relationship is interior, relational, provides real presence, requires two-way communication and is enduring.

By *interior* I mean that such knowledge has to be owned by each person in unique fashion. More than mere surface cordiality, a personal relationship should be able to answer such questions as "Who is this person for *me*?" and "What meaning does this relationship have for *me*?"

By *relational* I mean that, in healthy relationships, both parties need to be aware of the unique identity of the other and truly let the other *be* other. There should be no merging or confusion of identities. As with the mystery of the Trinity whose distinct relations with each other are the basis of their unity, so it is of true human relationship and genuine community.

Personal relationship also requires *presence*, which implies mutual and attentive awareness of each other. This kind of presence is more than physical. It can be presence-at-a-distance or presence-in-absence.

Personal relationship requires *mutual communication*. This calls for a sharing of self balanced with a respect for privacy. This means listening to and responding to each other. Such sharing includes not just external events, but also inner events such as thoughts and feelings, hopes and fears, successes and failures, sorrows and joys.

Genuine personal relationship has *durability* over time. It lasts through the "ups" and "downs" of affection. When love can't be *affective*, it can remain *effective* by "being there" and "doing for" the other. As with the mystery of the Trinity in whose image and likeness we're made, the love between devoted friends includes dimensions of self-giving, mutual and shared love.

I would suggest that the key to growth in devotional knowledge of the mysteries of faith is the cultivation of a contemplative attitude.

• How is your devotion to the mystery of the Trinity personal?

• How is it particular?

• How is it practical?

Chapter Five
Cultivating a
Contemplative Attitude

*B*y *"contemplative attitude" I mean one that pays attention to the religious dimensions of our everyday experience. Since God is present everywhere, all reality has a religious dimension that is available to any person of faith who can bring an attentive spirit to his/her own experience. A contemplative attitude is the mark of one who has a hospitable heart where there is space for God and other people.*

Someone has described contemplation as "taking a long, loving look at the real." I would suggest that, in the everyday activities of a busy life, we can also cultivate the habit of taking short glimpses!

To contemplate is to look lovingly, to listen deeply, to touch gently, to savor slowly, to become absorbed in someone or something outside self. It is to approach reality with reverence and awe rather than analysis and control.

A contemplative attitude is more receptive than active. More savoring than solving. More surrendering than achieving. More patient than hasty. More open than calculating. More playful than intense.

Perhaps a contemplative attitude is best expressed as being willing rather than being willful. A willing person freely chooses immersion in the process of life itself as participant rather than as observer. In contrast, a willful person sets herself or himself apart from life and attempts to master, control or otherwise manipulate it. In pursuing our desires, we must be willing, not willful.

Contemplation can be both "quiet" and "noisy." St. Teresa of Avila and St. John of the Cross are regarded as "quiet contemplatives." St. Vincent de Paul was a "noisy contemplative"; St. Louise de Marillac, a "busy mystic." For most of us, it need not be either Martha or Mary; rather it can be both/and. It was St. Augustine who said that no one should be so contemplative as to be unmindful of service to his or her neighbor; nor should he or she be so active as not to seek the contemplation of God. Contemplation is the womb from which deep compassion is born.

By "quiet" contemplation I mean emptying our minds and hearts to make hospitable and unambiguous space for the sheer mystery of the Trinity's indwelling presence. This allows the Spirit to speak in our silence and in our depths in a language beyond words and to translate our groanings into praise of the triune God. Spiritual disciplines helpful to "quiet" contemplation are silence and solitude. A striking example of "quiet" contemplation to which many modern pilgrims are being drawn today is centering prayer. More about that later.

"Noisy" contemplation seeks to build habits of contemplative prayer that can function in the ordinary circumstances of everyday life. Many find themselves in stressful, often hectic circumstances that seemingly would impair contemplation: homemaking, commuting in traffic, keeping schedules, making deadlines, etc. Bill Callahan of the Quixote Center indicates the value of noisy contemplation:

> By building contemplative habits throughout our daily lives, we can reach out in prayer to bond with God, with ourselves, and with our near and distant neighbors. By expanding our prayer to embrace all dimensions of the great commandment, praying becomes a way to integrate our lives so that we grow in faith, hope and love in the midst of our active, busy existence.[5]

Chief among the enemies of contemplation are self-absorption and "busy-ness."

Self-absorption is the opposite of contemplation which calls for getting out of oneself. Self-absorption can take many forms. Most obvious is getting "wrapped up" in

one's ego. Less obvious, but equally as unfriendly to contemplation, are self-absorption with one's guilt, wounds, resentments, anger, jealousy, etc. Each of these preoccupations simply crowds out the space in our consciousness that hospitality of the heart requires.

Another enemy of the hospitable heart is "busyness," that is, addiction to unreflective activity. This can masquerade as devotion or dedication, but, in effect, masks escape from intimacy with self, others and God. It can replace interpersonal relating, hamper communication, substitute activity for genuine service or ministry and lead to burnout.

• Can you recall a moment you've experienced in recent weeks when you were caught up in wonder, awe, reverence for someone or something outside yourself?

• Did it, in some way, heighten your awareness of God's presence?

• How do you balance "Martha and Mary" in your own journey of faith?

Chapter Six
A Path to Contemplation

*T*here is an ancient path to contemplation that continues to be helpful for many today. It is called lectio divina, a Latin term that literally means "divine reading." It is a way of praying reflectively with scripture especially, but is not limited to scripture. Many find it a helpful way of opening themselves to intimacy with God. It provides a hospitality of the heart for God's word spoken in scripture and God's word spoken elsewhere.

There are four steps on this path to contemplation: (1) reading, (2) meditation (reflection), (3) prayer (responding with words) and (4) contemplation (receiving without words). The movement on this path to God is from acquaintanceship (reading) to friendliness (meditation) to friendship (prayer) to intimacy or union (contemplation). They don't necessarily happen in this order. The sequence is just *our* need for keeping things neat. It's not necessarily *God's!* God is full of surprises and may break into our lives and prayer at any time. However, if nothing more, this sequence expresses our desire, our readiness, our invitation. It is helpful to prepare with a prayer asking for the grace to listen attentively to what God wants heard in this moment.

We begin then by *reading* a passage slowly and preferably aloud. As we listen to God's word, we try to notice and to savor words or phrases that seem to speak to us now.

Next we read the passage again, this time *reflecting*, searching for, but not forcing some meaning of what we've heard for our lives. What does God want us to hear at this time?

Once again we read the passage slowly and move to a *response* of prayer, letting our hearts speak to God honestly and spontaneously about what we're thinking and feeling.

We read the passage slowly a fourth time. Now we let go of all thoughts, words, feelings and images simply and quietly to rest in God *receptively*.

A simple way of looking at *lectio divina* is through the eyes of one country preacher who probably never heard of the Latin term. Nonetheless, when asked how he prayed, he summed it up in plain talk: "I reads myself full, thinks myself clear, prays myself hot and lets myself cool!"

First step: reading

Let's consider the first step of the *lectio* on the path to contemplation by selecting an episode of hospitality from the Old Testament. It is the story in Genesis about the visit of three strangers who bring the promise of a son to Abraham and Sarah.

We start by reading the text (Genesis 18:1–15) slowly, aloud and with attention. Pause to savor any word, phrase or verse that catches you. Don't force it. Let *it* catch you.

Next, we may want to allow other related biblical texts to expand the scope of this episode. The following are suggested texts with a sequence that may help. If others come to mind, go with them.

First we read Genesis 17:1–22 (another version of the same story) and Genesis 21 (the birth of Isaac).

We might want to read other Old Testament stories of a similar nature in which heavenly messengers are entertained unawares: Genesis 19:1–22 (Lot and his two angels); Judges 6:11–22 (Gideon's call by an angel); Tobit 5–12 (the adventures of Tobiah and Raphael).

We now can go to the New Testament to hear Jesus say that nothing is impossible with God: Matthew 19:26; Mark 10:27; Luke 1:37; 18:27.

We're ready now to move to passages from the

letters of St. Paul who holds up the faith of Abraham and Sarah as models to show that we are saved by faith, not good works: Romans 4:1–25; 9:6–9; Hebrews 11:8–19.

Next we can see a clear connection between the story in Genesis 18 and the plea for Christian hospitality: Hebrews 13:1–2.

You may find it helpful at this point to write your own version of the story. Here's my version. I've entitled it "Another Mysterious Threesome."

Abraham and Sarah had been called by God to leave their native land to embark on a long, arduous and uncertain journey of faith. Now the aging pilgrim and his barren wife had finally obtained property near Hebron where they could settle in an oak grove called Mamre near a cave named Machpelah. This was to be their permanent residence, their sanctuary and, eventually, their final resting place.

Can you imagine the scene described in chapter 18? The old patriarch is apparently praying or perhaps dozing in the heat of the day. Have you ever noticed how God seems to favor coming to people in their sleep as well as at prayer? Perhaps it's because we're less in control then!

Three strangers suddenly appear. With a spryness that belies his ninety-plus years, old Abraham springs to his feet to greet them with the customary bow of respect tendered by desert dwellers to visitors. After all, the host, not guest, is the honored one! Besides, it was common knowledge that Abraham took special delight in welcom-

ing guests. He and Sarah might be dubbed Old Testament "patron saints" of hospitality.

Surprisingly, Abraham now addresses his visitors in the singular. "My lord," he calls them. "Please do me the favor of staying for a while. You must be in need of refreshment and rest before you continue on your journey. I'll get some water for you to satisfy your thirst and to wash with. Please make yourself comfortable in the shade of that oak tree. After that, I'll get you a bite to eat. No doubt this is why you stopped."

Silent until now, one of the strangers replies, "We accept your welcome."

In an instant, old Abraham hobbles off to the tent to find Sarah. He says to her, "Quickly, prepare a new batch of bread and plenty of it." Then he hastens to his herd, selects his finest calf and instructs one of his hired hands to kill it and prepare it for roasting. When a hearty meal of milk, bread and veal is ready, Abraham himself serves it to his mysterious guests under the oak where they are resting. He stands nearby as hospitable host to perform this sacred duty.

After eating in silence, they (plural again!) question him about his wife. "Where is Sarah?" That takes him by surprise. He wonders, "How do they know her name?" It also frightens him a little. "What do they want with her, I wonder?" He knew that hospitality would demand that he grant whatever request his guests would make. "She's inside the tent," he answers nervously.

Then he is startled, not by a request, but by an

incredible promise. "When I (singular again!) come to visit you again next year, Sarah will have a son."

"Now that's a bit much!" he thinks.

In the meantime, Sarah has been standing out of sight behind the tent flap listening to the exchange. Aware of her faded beauty and vanished hopes of childbearing, she laughs to herself, not necessarily derisively or in disbelief, but perhaps at the incongruity of the promise. She doesn't yet know who the strangers are. She reddens with embarrassment when, apparently reading her thoughts, the stranger asks, "Is anything too great for Yahweh?" And he repeats, "When I visit again next year, Sarah will have a son."

"How did the stranger know I laughed?" Sarah thinks. Another mystery! Frightened, now she lies, "I didn't laugh," objecting defensively.

"Oh yes, you did," the divine visitor(s) replies.

You never know who's going to tug at the flap of your tent!

But Sarah had not been the first to laugh. So had Abraham in a previous version of the story. Nor is it Sarah's last laugh. After the ensuing birth of her son, she will say, "God has given me cause to laugh; all those who hear of it will laugh with me." So she names her son "Isaac" which means "God smiles."

• As you read the passage from Genesis, what word, phrase or verse especially caught your attention?

• As you heard yourself read, what new perspective, greater clarity or deeper self-understanding came to you?

• Who are some "Abrahams" or "Sarahs" who have modeled faith and trust in your life?

Chapter Seven
Second Step: Meditation

*T*his particular story of God's first appearance after the fall from grace draws upon a common folk-tale motif: *strangers who are treated hospitably come to be recognized as divine guests. The episode will become* the *paradigm for the Judeo-Christian tradition of hospitality. What began as hospitality of* hearth *for the divine messengers became hospitality of* heart *for their message.*

This passage from Genesis has provided biblical inspiration for a number of famous icons of the Holy Trinity. The most famous was done by a Russian monk from the fifteenth century, Andrei Rublev. I have found this icon a significant help in opening myself to a devotional knowledge of the mystery of the Most Holy Trinity. We'll continue this *lectio*, using the icon as the focal point for a reflection (meditation).

It would help if you had a copy of the icon at this time. If one is not available to you, I will attempt to create a "word picture" that may help you visualize the icon in your mind's eye. If you do have the icon, may I suggest a sequence of preparing to pray with it?

Preparation

Enthrone the icon.

Light a candle as a sign of the living presence of God.

Do some stretching and body prayer.

Sit and take an alert, yet relaxed posture before the icon.

Close your eyes and open your hands upward.

Take some slow, deep breaths.

Empty yourself of preoccupations, letting them go, one by one.

Find a word to regain your focus if your mind wanders; e.g., Abba, Jesus, Spirit.

Invite the triune God to be your special guest in this moment.

Pray your desire to be touched by God's triune presence and power.

You might chant softly or listen to a taped chant.

Icon of the Holy Trinity: a trinitarian window

As noted previously, Rublev (now Saint Andrei) found his biblical inspiration for the icon in the book of Genesis, chapter 18. This visit of the three strangers marks the beginning of the story of our salvation. Rublev painted the icon in honor of St. Sergius, patron saint of Russia (1313–1392). At a time of great turmoil in his country, St. Sergius had built a cathedral dedicated to the Holy Trinity in the midst of a forest. It was meant as a prayer that a world divided by hate would be filled with the love of the Trinity. He wanted to bring his country together around the name of God by contemplating the Holy Trinity. It was this prayer of sorrow and hope that Rublev rendered in paint.

This event had been interpreted by some fathers and doctors of the church and reflected in the popular piety of the early church as prefiguring the doctrine of the Trinity.

Word picture of the icon

In this "icon of icons," three Old Testament figures garbed in soft and majestic colors are depicted with heads bowed and forming a circle around a table. The circular formation is suggestive of the "eternal dance" of the Trinity. The three visitors in the icon have elongated bodies, are winged and haloed, feet not touching the ground suggesting they are more than human. Each holds a thin staff of equal length in hand, suggesting an equality among them. Yet the various colors of their garments, their postures and positions indicate that each is different and distinct.

On the table is a chalice containing a sacrificial offering suggesting a New Testament eucharistic setting. United at this table of sacrifice, they seem engaged in intimate communication and mutual concern. Their countenances reflect a sorrowful and compassionate, yet serene beauty. Many have identified the central figure as the Second Person of the Trinity. Part of his garment is reddish, and his hand, with two extended fingers raised over the cup of sacrifice, apparently signifies his human and divine natures as he engages in the eucharistic action.

There is an open space at the front of the table seemingly inviting the viewer to become part of their circle of compassionate love as partner in their "divine dance." Seemingly, viewers are invited to dwell in our own contemporary personal and societal turmoil of life with confidence and trust.

• You might pause at this point to be conscious of some of that turmoil that is part of your world at this time.

In the background of the icon, the home of Abraham and Sarah is depicted as a church. Hopefully it is one that welcomes a diversity of peoples, especially strangers, in a communion of love and celebration of eucharist.

• Has your experience of church been a welcoming one?

The oak of Mamre appears as a tree of life continuing and connecting with the life-giving sacrament on the table of sacrifice.

The icon seems to echo Jesus' priestly prayer: "I do not pray for them alone. I pray also for those who will believe in me through their word, that all may be one as you, Father, are in me and I in you; I pray that they may be one in us, that the world may believe that you sent me" (Jn 17:20–21).

Inside God's window

The icon's theology in color arose from Rublev's contemplation of contemporary events in human history in the light of the inspired word of God. It's a kind of "*lectio* in paint" that says a great deal to us about who God is and how God is involved in human affairs.

Trinity as relational and relevant

The icon depicts the Trinity as relational and having relevance for human history. Its historical biblical setting is at the home of Sarah and Abraham at the very beginning of salvation history. It likewise represents God's concern with contemporary human events at the time of St. Sergius. Rublev's intent in painting the icon was to portray the prayerful desire of St. Sergius—that the Holy Trinity would bring about a reflection of its divine life of love for a world divided by hate. The unity-in-diversity models God's desire for the whole of creation. There's also a sense of hope for the future as the eucharistic setting promises a heavenly banquet.

In finding his biblical inspiration from the event in Genesis, Rublev attempts to image a Trinity in which each person is distinct, but all united in a circle of love and engaged in a "divine dance." The God in whom we believe is one God with personal and communal dimensions. The icon is a rendition in color and form of the church's teaching of a triune God in which there is "union without confusion; distinction without separation."

The icon reveals something of the mystery of both the otherness and the closeness of the triune God in human history. God is certainly mysterious and elusive. Yet God is a personal presence to all of creation and its people whom God creates, saves and providently loves and cares for deeply and compassionately. Hardly distant and aloof, the God of our fathers and mothers is a God-for-us and a God-with-us.

The God we meet in the icon is one of surprises, coming to visit at unexpected times to unlikely people in ordinary human events, especially in transactions of human relationship. God comes as guest to bring blessing to those whose hearts and homes are hospitable. Abraham and Sarah welcome these divine visitors who, in turn, express God's welcome to this aging couple with the promise of an heir.

• Can you recall an occasion when God took you by surprise with an unexpected blessing?

This story of hospitality by Abraham and Sarah is the earliest in the Old Testament. Hospitality was a desert tradition inherited by the people of God. For nomadic tribes, it was a necessity. Considered sacred, guests were given refreshment and sanctuary. In a biblical sense, it came to have richer meaning. In offering generous welcome, especially to strangers, there comes a bonding and mutuality of exchange. In the exchange there comes for both guest and host the promise of new life. In any transaction of hospitality, the host is the honored one.

A tradition has it that this and other stories of hospitality concerning Abraham and Sarah circulated among the people. Their story left a religious mark on Jewish hospitality that will be further emphasized in later passages. There is a striking example in the book of Deuteronomy: "For the Lord, your God...executes justice for the orphan and the widow, and befriends the alien, feeding and clothing him. So you too must befriend the alien, for you were once aliens yourselves..." (Deut 10:17–19).

God calls people by name to indicate the specialness each has in God's sight. As with Abraham and Sarah, God sometimes changes names to indicate special missions in life.

God demonstrates a love for gatherings, especially for meals where there is unity and sharing. "Where two or three are gathered in my name, there am I in their midst" (Mt 18:20). God enters into intimate conversation with people and often questions them to draw out their deepest desires.

• Can you recall an occasion of gathering when God's presence seemed very real in the sharing?

Our God makes incredible promises and keeps them beyond our wildest expectations. Both Sarah and Abraham are beyond the age of childbearing. God brings more abundant life. Nothing is too great for God to accomplish. As a matter of fact, we are most vulnerable to God and grace in our weakness, our emptiness, our diminishments where God's power becomes more manifest.

• When have you found yourself more vulnerable to God in a situation of emptiness?

This icon speaks of God's genuine concern for us. The downward gaze of the three on the turmoil of St. Sergius' world communicates sadness and compassion.

Trinity as dynamic

The icon indicates that God is dynamic, not static. The figures are pictured in colors that shimmer, as strangers who travel and with movement that is circular. The unity of the Trinity is aesthetically realized through the harmony of color and circular movement of the persons toward each other and toward the eucharistic chalice in a "divine dance." The dynamism of the "divine dance" is mutual self-giving love.

Some have perceived the dynamism directed toward the eucharistic chalice as the mutual consent of the three to the incarnation and death of the Second Person so well expressed in the icon.[6] The icon can be seen as a meditation on the trinitarian implications of the text: "The Father loves me for this: that I lay down my life to take it up again...This command I received from my Father" (Jn 10:17).

The space at the table seems an invitation rather than a coercion to share trinitarian fellowship, to become "partners in the divine dance." Ours is a God who risks our refusal! In that sense, might we not attribute a "divine vulnerability" to the Godhead?

Our response

Our God expects a response of faith that enables us to trust in God's promises with attitudes of openness, risk and willing self-surrender, not willful control of our own destinies. God invites us to take our human experience—especially our relationships—seriously as privileged places of knowing God's presence, power, self-disclosure and limitless love.

God calls us to hospitality of home and heart, especially toward strangers who may come into our lives as divine visitors. Acts of hospitality would seem to be privileged places for fostering devotional knowledge of our three person'd God.

• What does either the passage from Genesis 18

or the icon say to you about who God is and how God is related to us?

- Who is the God of your experience?
- Can you recall an experience when you welcomed a stranger and received a surprise blessing?

Chapter Eight

Third Step: Prayer

Now that we've listened to the word and reflected on it, it's time to respond to the word by praying with it. We ask ourselves how God's word has spoken to our own experience of life. We ask how it affirmed or challenged us in some way. We get in touch with how it made us feel. Peaceful? Grateful? Hopeful? Lifted in spirit? Disturbed? Sorry? Inspired to do something good? Just happy and content to rest in God's presence? We try to get a sense of where our prayer seems to be leading us. We choose the kind of prayer to which the word now moves us. Praise? Contrition? Gratitude?

Intercession? Petition? Now is the time to say it from the heart. There are numerous options. Permit me to suggest a few.

Quiet prayer with the icon

Take a close look at the icon, noticing the eyes especially.

Keep your eyes still. Let yourself be known by God through the eyes of the icon.

Let the eyes of the icon become your eyes.

Gently release any sense of judgment, hardness, curiosity, mistrust that may arise.

Open yourself for God to bring whatever healing, illumination, inspiration that might come.

Be still as you spend time with the icon.

Praying with parables

Praying with parables calls for a special kind of *lectio*. Perhaps you will find some of the following considerations helpful.

Remember...

The parable is not a finished story. It's never told the same way twice. Each parable has to be seen within the context of the other parables. To pray a parable, a person must get involved with it and be questioned by it. It is as if one is on the edge of a crowd trying to hear Jesus. He or she tries to get closer to listen. The parable should lead to choice, either to accept or to reject any invitation it extends. A decision to accept the invitation can bring a new vision and a changed life.

The essential message in all the parables is that the reign of God is here and that we can experience that message through the medium of the parable. It makes happen what it describes. Each parable is a mini-gospel. The result of hearing hopefully will be a joyful response to the good news it proclaims.

There are three moments in a parable: (1) revelation: a story sets up possibilities; (2) revolution: one's world is turned around; (3) resolution: some decision is made.

So get ready...

What event in your life seems to be drawing you that you either are finding exciting or are perhaps rejecting? Where is your energy being used either in pursuit or in flight? Tell yourself a story of what's happening to you.

Go...

Read the parable slowly, aloud and attentively. Look for one point. Don't try to tie down all the details. Surrender yourself to the word. Let it affect you. Let it do the work. Let it take over control. Let it find its own focus.

You might pray with one of the following parables to find connections with Genesis 18:

> Matthew 13:44-46 (The Treasure and the Pearl)
> Matthew 22:1-14; Luke 14:16-24 (The Banquet)
> Luke 10:29-37 (The Good Samaritan)
> Mark 4:26-29 (The Patient Farmer)

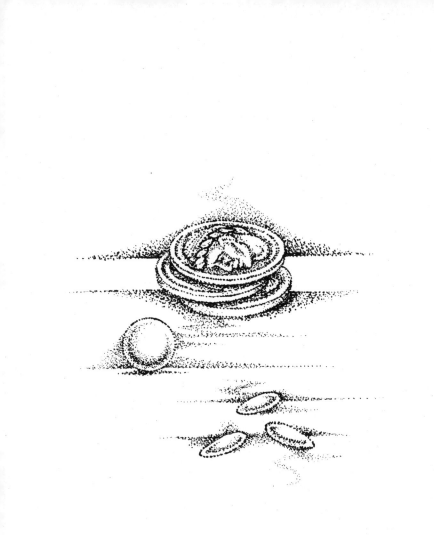

Mark 4:30–32; Matthew 13:31–32; Luke 13:18–19 (The Mustard Seed)

• What connection did you find with the story in Genesis?

• With whom do you identify in the parable? How are you like that person?

• What change do you find yourself wanting to pursue or resist?

Another option would be to imagine you are an invited guest filling the empty seat at the table in the icon and sharing the divine conversation. You might simply say in our own words how the time spent with our three person'd God at this time has made you feel. In your conversation, it might be revealing to ask such questions as, "Lord, when did we see you hungry and feed you or see you thirsty and give you drink? When did we welcome you away from home or clothe you in your nakedness? When did we visit you when you were ill or in prison?" (Mt 25:37–39).

Or perhaps you would prefer to pray a psalm that expresses what you feel. For example, you may find Psalm 139 a fine expression of the intimate presence and personal concern of an all-knowing God; Psalm 51 as a profound expression of repentance; Psalm 88 as a fitting lament in times of affliction; etc.

Another option would be to choose another of your favorite prayers that has meaning for the moment.

For example, a prayer of abandonment or "letting go" such as those of St. Ignatius Loyola, Mother Catherine McAuley or Little Brother Charles de Foucauld.

Closing prayer with the icon

Take some time to express gratitude and praise to the triune God for all the icons in your life.

Acknowledge any blindness due to personal cares, concerns, hurts or prejudices that may have blocked God's presence and power through others in your life.

Chapter Nine
Fourth Step: Contemplation

W e have arrived at the final step of our prayer journey. It's time to let go of our previous activity and just "be" in the presence of our three person'd God to receive.

I have a cartoon that pictures two eastern monks, robed and unshod, sitting side by side in position for prayer. The younger, apparently a novice at this kind of prayer, looks somewhere between confusion and frustration. The elder is saying, "Nothing comes next. This is it."

The cartoon reminds me of my own younger novice days at prayer. Early on, a spiritual mentor had urged me to a practice of the presence of God in my life, largely by thinking and imaging. I have since learned that this ancient practice has its source in Paul's words to the Athenians, "In him we live and move and have our being" (Acts 17:28). Long present in the Christian tradition, I once again find it clearly expressed in the writings of St. Francis de Sales. He elaborates different ways of placing ourselves in God's presence. One of them is "to remember that (God) is present in a most particular manner in your heart and in the center of your spirit."[7] That's the "celibate core" to which I referred earlier. It's also the place of "quiet" contemplation.

Despite my introduction to this hallowed tradition of contemplation by mentor and classical masters, my recollection is that not much "happened next" for me save confusion and frustration! The trouble was I tried too hard. At best, my mind would wrap itself around some philosophical notion of God's omnipresence or my imagination would conjure up a holy card image. At worst, I'd engage in near compulsive attempts to remain in God's presence by the desperate repetition of ejaculatory prayers. Not surprisingly, my practice waned and I drifted in more rewarding directions where something did seem to "happen next."

In my later "novice" years, another spiritual mentor nudged me once again toward the practice with another "spin." It's called "centering prayer." Also deeply rooted in the spiritual tradition of the west as well as the east, the approach is somewhat different. It's prayer of quiet and presence rather than words and activity. Now (on my more fervent days!), heeding the words of the psalmist, "Be still and confess that I am God" (Ps 46:11), I let myself enter into the mystery of God already present at the center (and the circumference) of my being. Now (again, on my better days!), it's more on God's terms than mine. In some ways, this prayer resembles that of the monks in the cartoon. But there are profound differences. It's not true that "nothing happens next." Often I hear the objection that this kind of prayer is not Christian. My response: It is Christian to the extent that it is trinitarian, that is, deeply rooted in baptismal identity. It can lay claim to that by what "happens" after and especially what "happens" before the time of prayer. I'd like to suggest some trinitarian dimensions that might precede and follow quiet centering prayer.

What happens before is nourishment of the deep intention I bring to my prayer. It's always to God through Christ in the Holy Spirit.

One person can be moved by different intentions. For example, the same person can visit as *salesperson* to sell, as *patron* to grant a favor, as *minister* to provide spiritual help, or simply as *friend* to be with. In each case, the visit will have different meanings for both visitor and visited.

In similar fashion, I can approach centering with different deep intentions. The possibilities include: (1) a search for the bliss of Nirvana (operative I would guess in the cartoon, at least for the elder monk!); (2) a search for deeper union within self for relaxation, better concentration or an altered state of consciousness; (3) a search for deeper union with the world of nature or people; (4) a search for deeper union with transcendent reality that can range from vague awareness of a "higher power" to a three person'd God.

Quiet centering prayer would seem a most appropriate expression of deep trinitarian intention. It is elegant silent testimony to the claim of Paul: "The life I live now is not my own; Christ is living in me" (Gal 2:20).

In terms of what "happens next," as with all authentic prayer, the expected outcome is growth in the love of God and others. Along with growth in love, we might also expect an outpouring of love's companion gift, wisdom. Jesuit William Johnston says, "Progress in charity ...means progress in wisdom. This kind of wisdom is...apparent in human relations where love can discover beauty and potentiality that reason alone cannot find."[8]

In addition, we might also expect a maturing of the fruits of the Holy Spirit to become evident in our lives: love, joy, peace, patience, kindness, goodness, trustfulness, gentleness and self-control. This maturing, in turn, should lead to deeper and wider compassion. As I said previously, contemplation is the womb from which compassion is born. Cistercian Basil Pennington says how this happens:

> The way the Holy Spirit seems to bring this about...is that in this prayer we experience not only our oneness with God in Christ, but also our oneness with all the rest of the Body of Christ and, indeed, with the whole of creation, in

God's creative love and sharing in being. Thus we begin...to experience the presence of God in all things, the presence of Christ in each person we meet...From this flows a true compassion—a "feeling with."[9]

To the extent that quiet centering prayer is trinitarian, Christ's attitudes and beatitudes can become more our own. One might expect a greater ease in surrendering to God's desires. Though prayer in its own right, this can also dispose us for experiencing the presence of God in other forms of prayer such as the liturgy of the hours.

The quiet, peace and willingness can begin to "ripple" through the rest of life and its daily activities. It might well bring about a more gentle and loving practice of ministry.

As for the actual experience of quiet centering prayer, what hopefully "happens" is implied in the adjective "centering." This is a term potters use for the act that precedes all the others on the potter's wheel. It is the act of bringing the clay into a spinning, unwobbling pivot. This frees the clay to take innumerable shapes as potter and clay press against each other. The potter touches the clay at only one point, yet as the pot turns in the potter's hands, the whole vessel is affected. There is an experience of wholeness. So it is with quiet centering prayer. The object is not to "wobble." Let the Potter do the work!

It is my conviction that willing fidelity (rather than willful effort) over time to a discipline of spending unam-

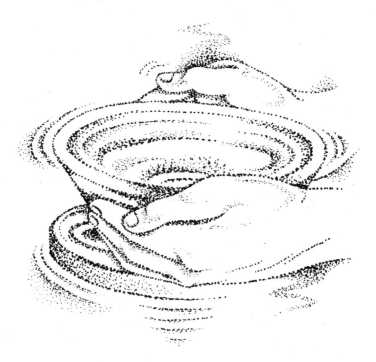

biguous time at the Potter's wheel is body language saying where we want our hearts to be. In these later "novice" efforts at the practice of the presence of God, even as I "wobble," Jeremiah's visit to the potter comforts me:

> This word came to Jeremiah from the Lord: Rise up, be off to the potter's house; there I will give you my message. I went down to the potter's house and there he was, working at the wheel. Whenever the object of clay which he was making turned out badly in his hand, he tried again, making of the clay another object of whatever sort he pleased. Then the word of the Lord came to me: Can I not do to you, house of Israel, as this potter has done? says the Lord. Indeed, like clay in the hand of the potter, so are you in my hand, house of Israel (Jer 18:1–6).

Journaling

• Was there any graced moment that revealed something significant for your way of seeing and being during this time?

• Have there been any objects, persons, places or events that have been special icons for you in the past?

• How have they revealed the compassionate presence and power of God by illuminating, inspiring, transforming, loving you?

* * *

Follow-up

As a follow-up to this time of prayer, you might continue prayerful awareness with your eyes. Let all become icons, transparencies of God for you. Keep making yourself available for God's presence throughout the day.

You might also hold in consciousness some scripture passage that can help keep you available for God's presence such as:

"O Lord, you have probed me and you know me..." (Ps 139).

"We do not fix our gaze on what is seen, but on what is unseen" (2 Cor 4:18).

"My being proclaims the greatness of the Lord..." (Lk 1:46).

"I am the good shepherd. I know my sheep and my sheep know me in the same way that the Father knows me and I know the Father" (Jn 10:14–15).

Conclusion

I t seems right to conclude this little "dance" with a prayer to the Trinity composed by one of my favorite prayer partners. We companioned one another on our faith journeys for the last twenty-three years of her life. Always hosting God in her heart during her earthly sojourn, Sister "Sarah" was received as guest in the place Jesus went ahead to prepare for her at the age one hundred and three. We're still part-ners, of course. She used to pray for all my com-ings and goings and the people to whom I would minister. She assured me that she'd be in an even better position to do that after she moved on. I invite you to share our prayer:

Father, draw us to Jesus.
Jesus, show us the Father's love.
Holy Spirit, consecrate us
in the Truth.
O Most Holy Trinity,
accomplish your desires in us
that we may be one with you
and share your joy. Amen.

Afterword

Continuing in Step with the Divine Dance

I *can't imagine this divine "dance card"*
ever filled up or the dance ever finished.
So I would urge us all to continue to be
"in step" (and even to learn some new steps!) as
we worship attentively together, as we live harmo-
niously in a communion of faith and as we reflec-
tively pray the scriptures.

     As we join in worship, let's be especially attentive
to the doxology that concludes the eucharistic prayer and
precedes the Lord's Prayer: "Through him, with him, in
him, in the unity of the Holy Spirit, all glory and honor is
yours, almighty Father, forever and ever."

• With Jesus as mediator, neither he nor we stand alone before the Father in praise. Both he and we as partners are together in praise.

• Bespeaking the reality of the triune God, this prayer shows the relationship of the Holy Spirit to each of us and all of us. It is by the power of the Holy Spirit that each of us is empowered to confess Jesus as Lord (1 Cor 12:3) and to claim God as "Abba" (Rom 8:15). That same Holy Spirit is the author of our unity and communion as church which we affirm in the response, "Amen!"

As we live together in a communion of faith, we might reflect on such prayers as the alternative one in the mass for Trinity Sunday: "God, we praise you...You reveal yourself in the depths of our being, drawing us to share in your life and love. One God, three persons, be near to the people formed in your image, close to the world your love brings to life..."

• In praying these words, consider how all truly Christian prayer is solidary rather than solitary.

• Commit yourself more deeply to living in a community of faith that reflects the communitarian life of God.

As we read the sacred scriptures, we might prayerfully reflect on those passages especially from the gospel of John and the letters of Paul that make the mystery of the triune God accessible. Those passages are most powerful that reveal the Incarnate Word as one whose sacrificial love for us is most evident in his passion and death on the cross.

• In God's giving us his only Son (Jn 3:16), we experience Jesus as the icon of the triune God whose life is perfect love that is self-giving, mutual and shared. This love and this life make the "divine dance" possible for us who live in a world plagued by suffering because the three divine persons have made human history part of their own divine life.

• Knowing that God is for us (Rom 8:31) is dramatically revealed in the passion and death of Jesus. Through the cross, we are created anew, redeemed and sanctified.

• Though he returns to the Father, Jesus does not do so before promising to send us another advocate—one who is distinct but equal (Jn 14:16; 16:7); one who will remind us of all Jesus taught and who will lead us to complete truth (Jn 14:26; 16:13ff.); one whom we will experience in the distribution of a variety and unity of spiritual gifts (1 Cor 12:1–11). With, through and in the fellowship of this Spirit, the love and saving grace of Jesus, we are called to be partners in the divine dance.

May we always step lively!

Notes

1. A reflection on spiritual community written at the Shalem Institute for Spiritual Formation Residency, June 1990, by Shirley Cunningham.

2. Cf. Catherine de Hueck Doherty, *Poustinia* (Notre Dame, IN: Ave Maria Press, 1975).

3. Robert Fulghum, *All I Really Need to Know I Learned in Kindergarten* (New York: Ivy Books, 1986), pp. 54–56.

4. St. Francis de Sales, *Introduction to a Devout Life* (Garden City, NY: Image Books, 1972), pp. 40–41.

5. W.R. Callahan, *Noisy Contemplation* (Hyattsville, MD: Quixote Center, 1982), p. 5.

6. J. McDade, "The Trinity and the Paschal Mystery," *Heythrop Journal* XXIX (1988), pp. 175–191.

7. Op. cit., pp. 84ff.

8. William Johnston, ed., *The Cloud of Unknowing and the Book of Privy Counseling* (Garden City, NY: Image Books, 1973), p. 20.

9. B. Pennington, *Finding Grace at the Center* (Still River, MA: St. Bede Publications, 1978), p. 20.

ILLUMINATIONBOOKS

Other Books in the Series

Little Pieces of Light...Darkness and Personal Growth
   by Joyce Rupp

Lessons from the Monastery That Touch Your Life
   by M. Basil Pennington, O.C.S.O.

As You and the Abused Person Journey Together
   by Sharon E. Cheston

Spirituality, Stress & You
   by Thomas E. Rodgerson

Joy, The Dancing Spirit of Love Surrounding You
   by Beverly Elaine Eanes

Why Are You Worrying?
   by Joseph W. Ciarrocchi

Celebrating the Woman You Are
   by S. Suzanne Mayer, I.H.M.

Every Decision You Make Is a Spiritual One
   by Anthony J. De Conciliis with John F. Kinsella

Love God...Clean House...Help Others
   by Duane F. Reinert, O.F.M. Cap.